PLAY DRUMS WITH

THE BEST OF
AC/DC

PLAY DRUMS WITH

THE BEST OF
AC/DC

Wise Publications
part of The Music Sales Group
London / New York / Paris / Sydney / Copenhagen / Berlin / Madrid / Tokyo

Published by
Wise Publications
14-15 Berners Street, London W1T 3LJ, UK

Exclusive Distributors:
Music Sales Limited
Distribution Centre, Newmarket Road,
Bury St Edmunds, Suffolk IP33 3YB, UK

Music Sales Pty Limited
20 Resolution Drive,
Caringbah, NSW 2229, Australia

Order No. AM1000406
ISBN 978-1-84938-515-2
This book © Copyright 2010 Wise Publications,
a division of Music Sales Limited.

Printed in the EU

www.musicsales.com

Compiled by Nick Crispin
Music arranged by Paul Townsend
Edited by Adrian Hopkins
Music processed by Paul Ewers Music Design

CD recorded, mixed and mastered by Jonas Persson
Additional progamming by Rick Cardinali
All guitars by Arthur Dick
Bass by Tom Farncombe
Drums by Noam Lederman

DRUM KIT NOTATION KEY

The following system of drum kit notation is employed in this book:

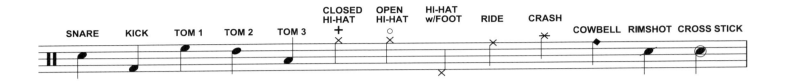

BACK IN BLACK

WORDS & MUSIC BY
ANGUS YOUNG, MALCOLM YOUNG & BRIAN JOHNSON

FULL PERFORMANCE DEMO: CD 1 TRACK 1
BACKING ONLY: CD 2 TRACK 1

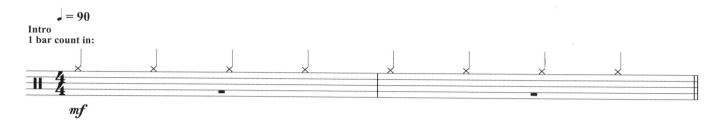

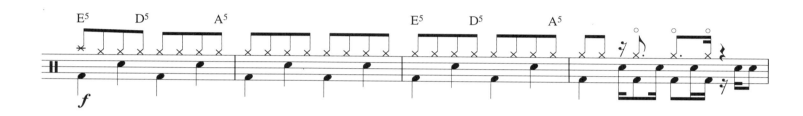

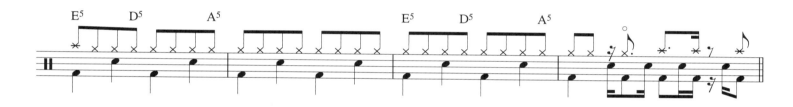

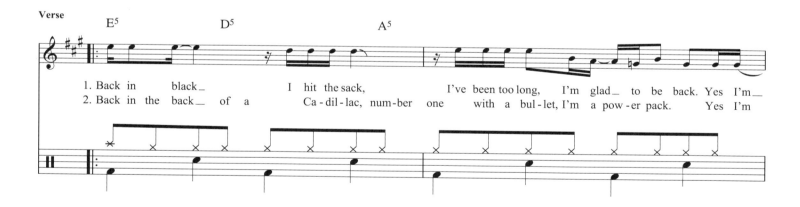

1. Back in black __ I hit the sack, I've been too long, I'm glad __ to be back. Yes I'm
2. Back in the back __ of a Ca-dil-lac, num-ber one with a bul-let, I'm a pow-er pack. Yes I'm

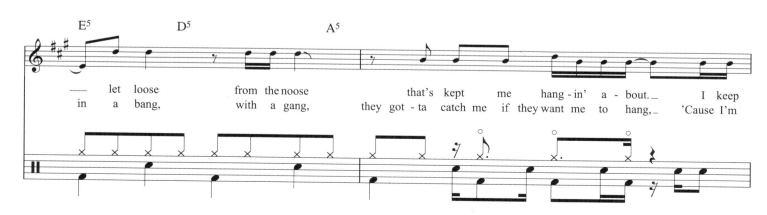

— let loose from the noose that's kept me hang-in' a-bout. __ I keep
in a bang, with a gang, they got-ta catch me if they want me to hang, __ 'Cause I'm

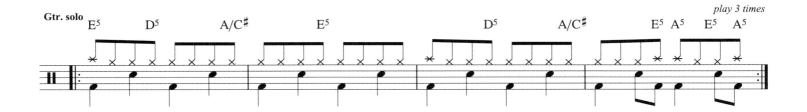

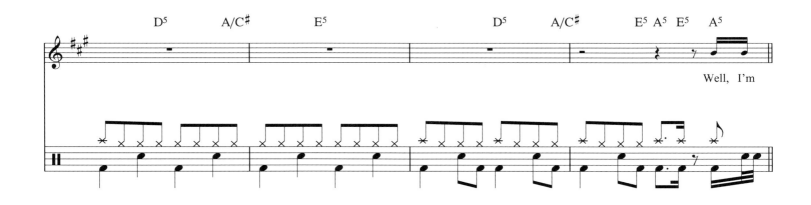

10

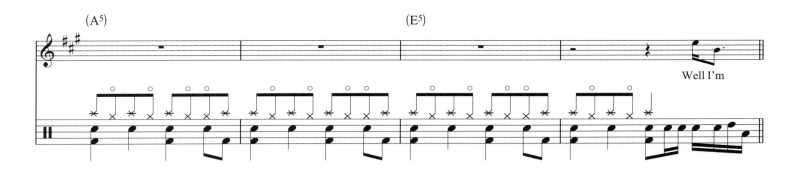

Well I'm

Chorus A⁵ E⁵ B⁵ A⁵ B⁵ A⁵ E⁵ B⁵ A⁵ B⁵ G⁵ D⁵ A⁵ G⁵ D⁵ A⁵

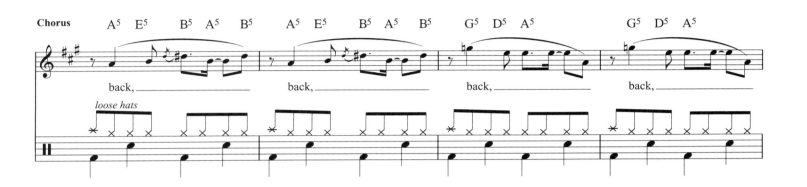

back, _____ back, _____ back, _____ back, _____

loose hats

E⁵ B⁵ A⁵ B⁵ A⁵ E⁵ B⁵ A⁵ G⁵

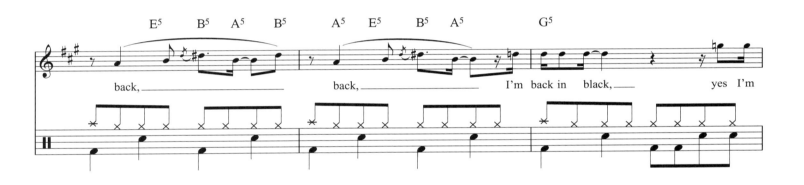

back, _____ back, _____ I'm back in black, _____ yes I'm

D⁵ A⁵

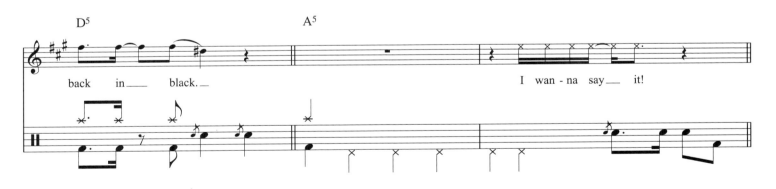

back in _____ black. _____ I wan - na say _____ it!

Repeat to fade

E⁵ D⁵ A/C♯ E⁵ D⁵ A/C♯ E⁵ A⁵ E⁵ A⁵

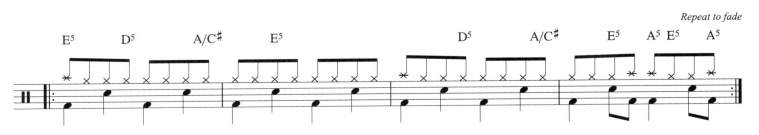

DIRTY DEEDS DONE DIRT CHEAP

WORDS & MUSIC BY
ANGUS YOUNG, MALCOLM YOUNG & BON SCOTT

FULL PERFORMANCE DEMO: CD 1 TRACK 2
BACKING ONLY: CD 2 TRACK 2

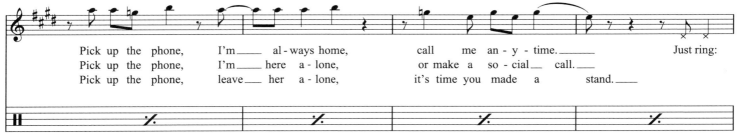

Pick up the phone, I'm_____ al-ways home,   call   me an-y-time._____   Just ring:
Pick up the phone, I'm_____ here a-lone,   or make a so-cial_____ call._____
Pick up the phone, leave_____ her a-lone,   it's time you made a   stand._____

To Coda ⊕

three six two_____ four   three six   o,_____   I lead a life   of crime._____
Come right in,   for-get a-bout him,   we'll have our-selves a   ball._____
For a fee,_____ I'm hap-py to be   your   back door   man._____ Ooh!

1,3°

2°

Chorus   A⁵   G⁵   A⁵   E⁵   D⁵   E⁵

Dirt - y deeds   done dirt cheap.   Dirt - y deeds   done dirt cheap.

loose hats

f

A⁵   G⁵   A⁵   E⁵

Dirt - y deeds   done dirt cheap.   Dirt - y deeds and they're done   dirt cheap.

1.   D⁵   **2.**

Dirt - y deeds_____ and they're done   dirt cheap.   done dirt cheap.

FOR THOSE ABOUT TO ROCK (WE SALUTE YOU)

WORDS & MUSIC BY
ANGUS YOUNG, MALCOLM YOUNG & BRIAN JOHNSON

FULL PERFORMANCE DEMO: CD 1 TRACK 3
BACKING ONLY: CD 2 TRACK 3

Verse

Stand up and be count - ed for what you are a - bout to re - ceive.___

We are the deal - ers, we'll give you ev -'ry-thing you need. ___

Verse

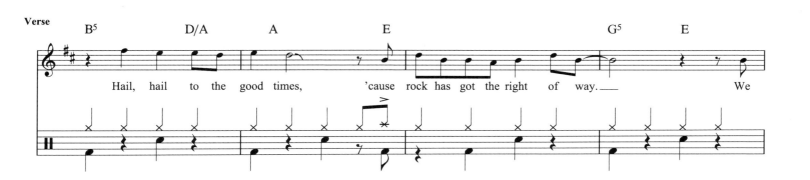

Hail, hail to the good times, 'cause rock has got the right of way. ___ We

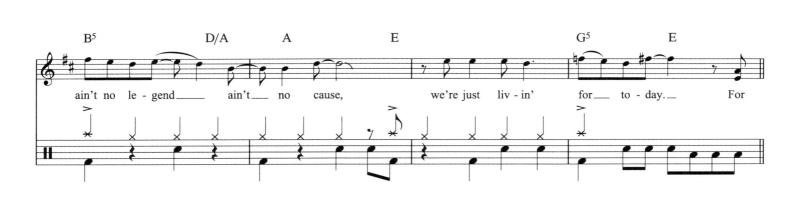

ain't no le - gend ___ ain't ___ no cause, we're just liv - in' for ___ to - day. ___ For

Chorus

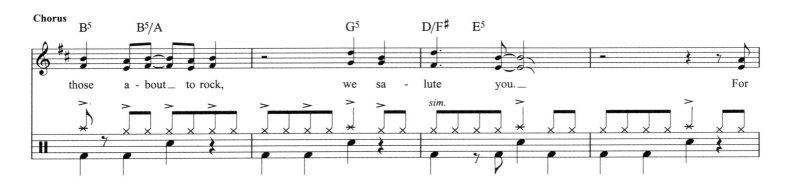

those a - bout ___ to rock, we sa - lute you.___ For

17

those a - bout to rock, we sa - lute you. 3. We

Verse

rock at dawn on the front line, like a bolt right - a out of the blue. The

sky's a - light with a gui - tar bite, heads will roll and rock to - night. For

Chorus

those a - bout to rock, we sa - lute you. For

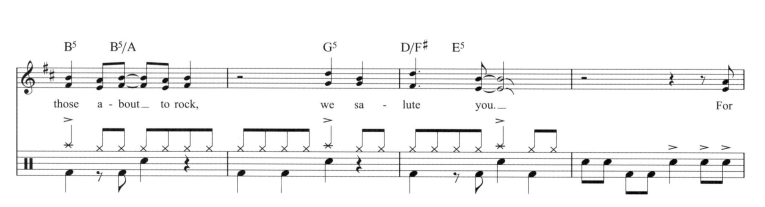

those a - bout to rock, we sa - lute you. For

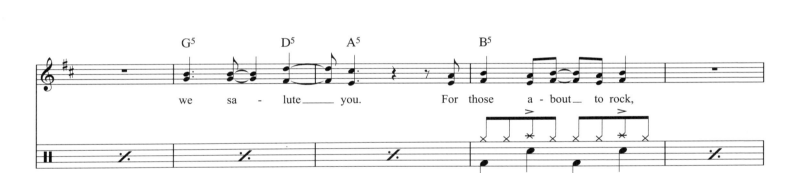

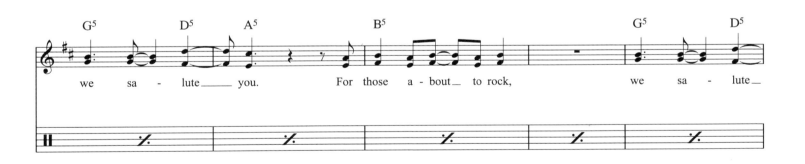

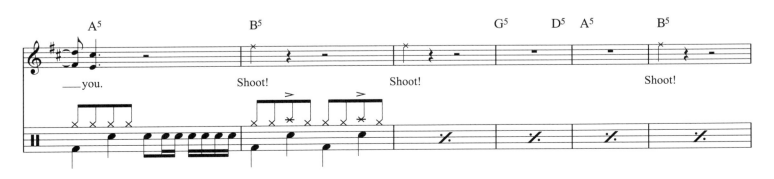

HELLS BELLS

WORDS & MUSIC BY
ANGUS YOUNG, MALCOLM YOUNG & BRIAN JOHNSON

FULL PERFORMANCE DEMO: CD 1 TRACK 4
BACKING ONLY: CD 2 TRACK 4

Verse

1. I'm roll - in' thun - der, _____ pour - in' rain,
(2.) black sen - sa - tions up and down your spine,

I'm com - in' on like a hur - ri - cane. _____ See my
if you're in - to ev - il, you're a friend of mine. _____ See my

My light - nin's flash - in' _____ a - cross the sky,
white light flash - in' as I split the night, 'cause if

you're on - ly young but you're gon - na die. _____ I _____
good's on the left _____ then I'm stick - in' to the right. _____

Pre-chorus

_____ won't take no pri - son - ers, won't _____ spare no lives, _____

2. (A⁵)

Yow!

Gtr. solo

A⁵ ‖ C⁵ ‖ D⁵ ‖ A⁵ ‖ C⁵ ‖ D⁵

A⁵ ‖ C⁵ ‖ D⁵ ‖ A⁵ ‖ C⁵ ‖ D⁵

C⁵ G⁵ ‖ D⁵ ‖ C⁵ G⁵

E⁵ ‖ D⁵ A⁵ ‖ E⁵ ‖ G⁵

Hell's

Chorus

A⁵ ‖ Asus⁴ ‖ Am⁷ ‖ Asus⁴ ‖ A⁵ ‖ Asus⁴ ‖ Am⁷ ‖ Asus⁴ ‖ C⁵ ‖ G/B

bells, __ Sa - tan's call-ing to you, __ Hell's bells. __ He's ring-in' 'em now, Hell's

26

HIGHWAY TO HELL

WORDS & MUSIC BY
ANGUS YOUNG, MALCOLM YOUNG & BON SCOTT

FULL PERFORMANCE DEMO: CD 1 TRACK 5
BACKING ONLY: CD 2 TRACK 5

IT'S A LONG WAY TO THE TOP (IF YOU WANNA ROCK 'N' ROLL)

WORDS & MUSIC BY
ANGUS YOUNG, MALCOLM YOUNG & BON SCOTT

FULL PERFORMANCE DEMO: CD 1 TRACK 6
BACKING ONLY: CD 2 TRACK 6

get-tin' stoned, ___ get-tin' beat ___ up, bro-ken bones. ___ Get-tin' had, __

(12)

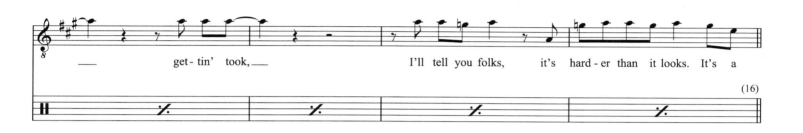

get-tin' took, ___ I'll tell you folks, it's hard-er than it looks. It's a

(16)

Chorus

A⁵　　　　　G⁵　　　D/F♯　　A⁵

long　way　to the top ___ if you wan-na rock 'n' roll, ___　　　　it's a

A⁵　　　　　G⁵　　　D/F♯　　A⁵

long　way　to the top ___ if you wan-na rock 'n' roll. ___　　　　If you

A⁵　　　　　　　　　　　　D/A

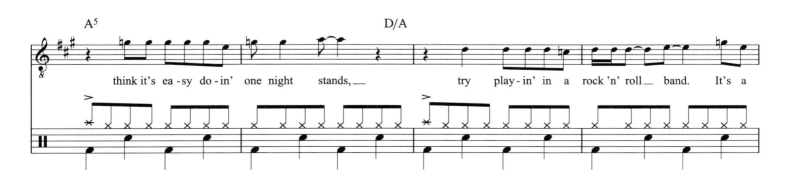

think it's ea-sy do-in' one night　stands, ___　try play-in' in a rock 'n' roll __ band.　It's a

33

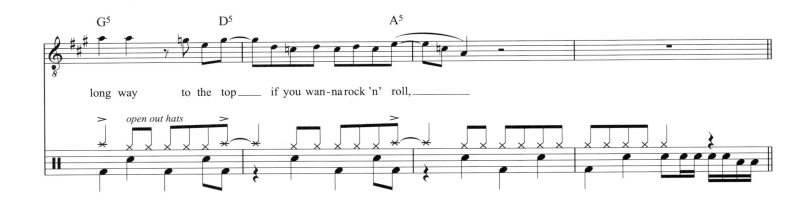

long way   to the top_____ if you wan-na rock 'n' roll,_____

Interlude (bagpipes)

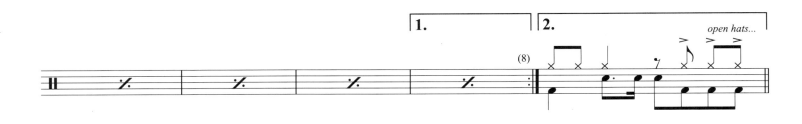

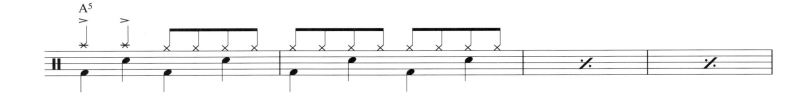

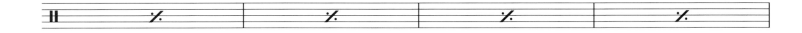

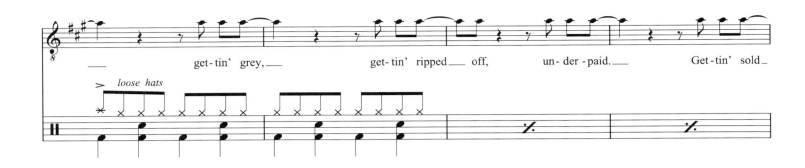

get-tin' grey,___ get-tin' ripped___ off, un-der-paid.___ Get-tin' sold_

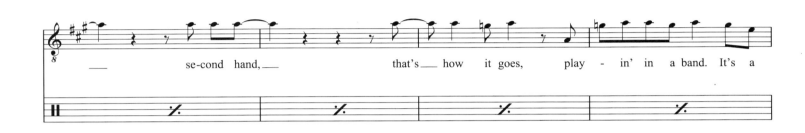

se-cond hand,___ that's__ how it goes, play-in' in a band. It's a

Chorus

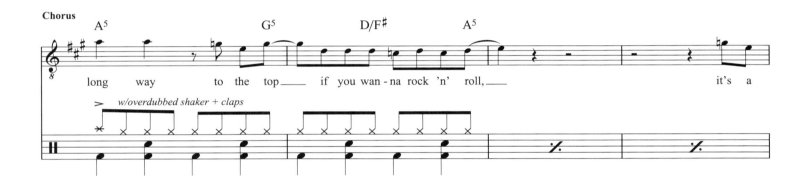

long way to the top___ if you wan-na rock 'n' roll,___ it's a

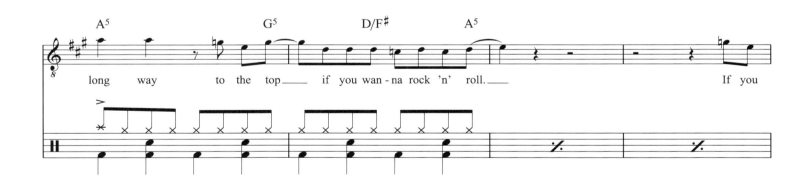

long way to the top___ if you wan-na rock 'n' roll.___ If you

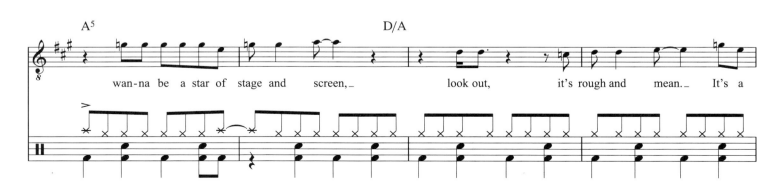

wan-na be a star of stage and screen,_ look out, it's rough and mean._ It's a

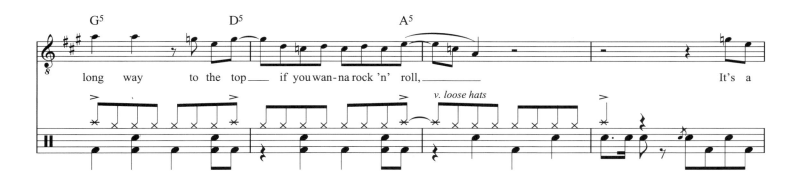

long way to the top___ if you wan-na rock 'n' roll, ___ It's a

long way to the top___ if you wan-na rock 'n' roll. ___

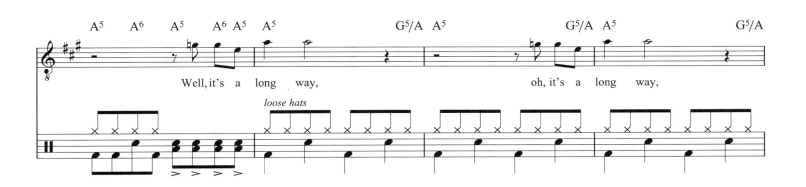

Well, it's a long way, oh, it's a long way,

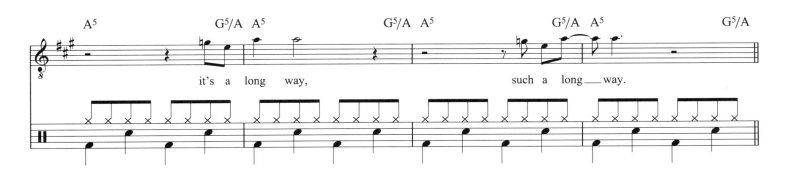

it's a long way, such a long___ way.

Repeat ad lib. to fade

Outro

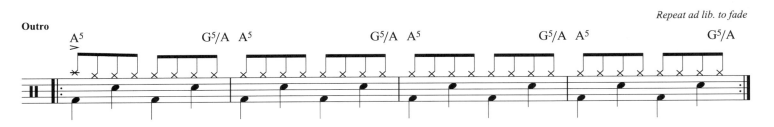

LET THERE BE ROCK

WORDS & MUSIC BY
ANGUS YOUNG, MALCOLM YOUNG & BON SCOTT

FULL PERFORMANCE DEMO: CD 1 TRACK 7
BACKING ONLY: CD 2 TRACK 7

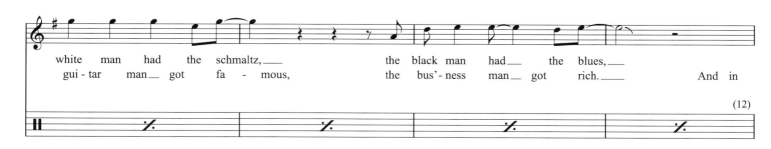

no - one knew what they was gon - na do ___ but Tchai - kov - sky had ___ the news. He said, "Let there be sound," ___
ev - 'ry bar ___ there was a su - per - star _____ with a sev - en year ___ itch. There were

(16)

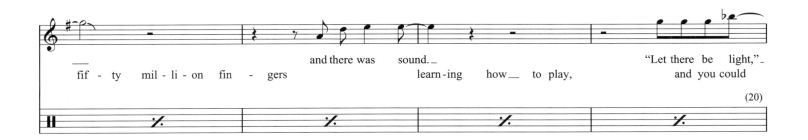

___ and there was sound. ___ "Let there be light," ___
fif - ty mil - li - on fin - gers learn - ing how ___ to play, and you could

(20)

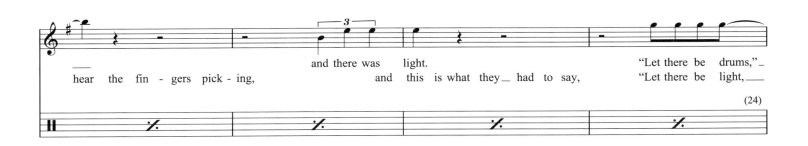

and there was light. "Let there be drums," ___
hear the fin - gers pick - ing, and this is what they ___ had to say, "Let there be light, ___

(24)

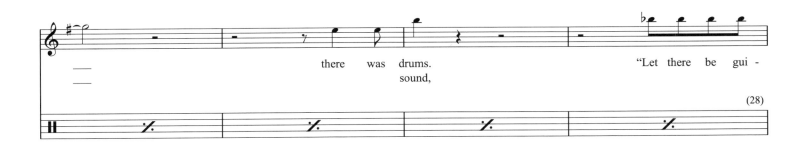

there was drums. "Let there be gui -
sound, ___

(28)

To Coda ⊕

A⁵

- tar," there was gui - tar. _____ Oh, _____ let there be rock.
drums, gui - tar."

open out

ff

39

Gtr. solo

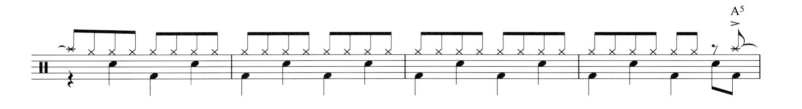

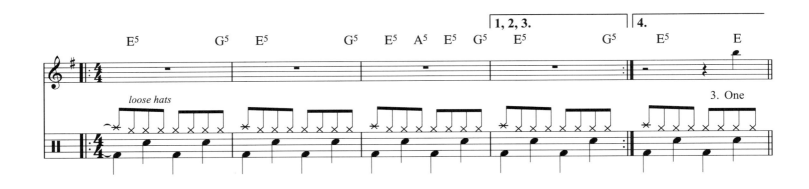

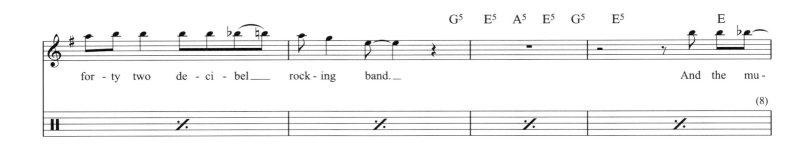

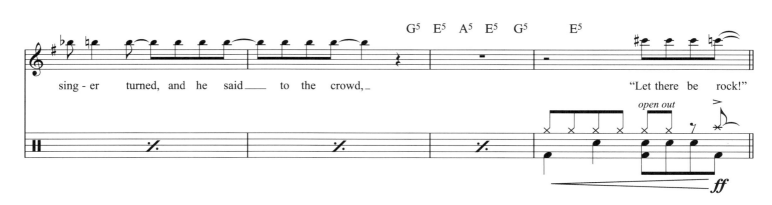

Chorus

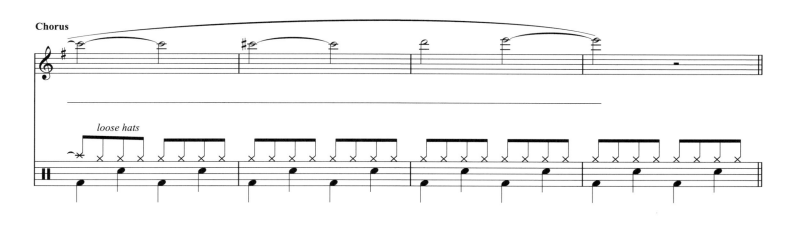

loose hats

Gtr. solo

|1-4.| |5.| B⁵

(20)

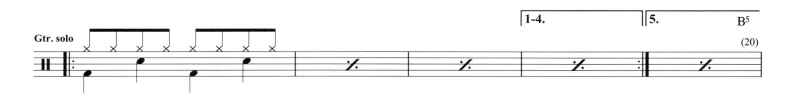

B

(28)

Play 3 times

Freely

B   E   B

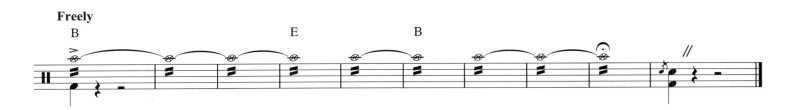

ROCK AND ROLL AIN'T NOISE POLLUTION

WORDS & MUSIC BY
ANGUS YOUNG, MALCOLM YOUNG & BRIAN JOHNSON

FULL PERFORMANCE DEMO: CD 1 TRACK 8
BACKING ONLY: CD 2 TRACK 8

Intro
2 bar count in:
♩ = 90

1. Hey there all you middle men, throw away your fancy clothes.
2. Because rock 'n' roll ain't no riddle man. To me it makes

sittin' on a fence. So get off your arse and come down here.
good, good sense, (2.) good sense, yeah let's go.

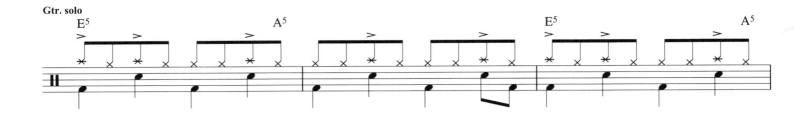

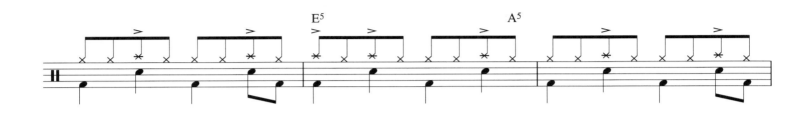

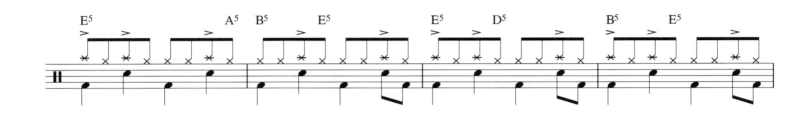

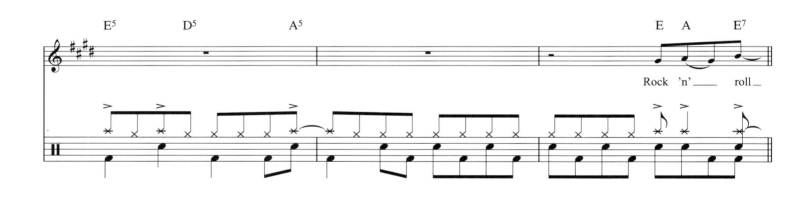

Rock 'n'___ roll___

Chorus

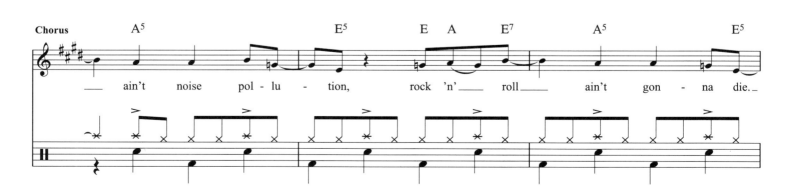

___ ain't noise pol - lu - tion, rock 'n'___ roll___ ain't gon - na die._

ROCK 'N' ROLL TRAIN

WORDS & MUSIC BY
ANGUS YOUNG & MALCOLM YOUNG

FULL PERFORMANCE DEMO: CD 1 TRACK 9
BACKING ONLY: CD 2 TRACK 9

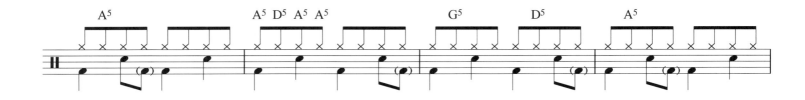

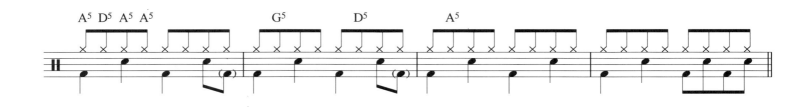

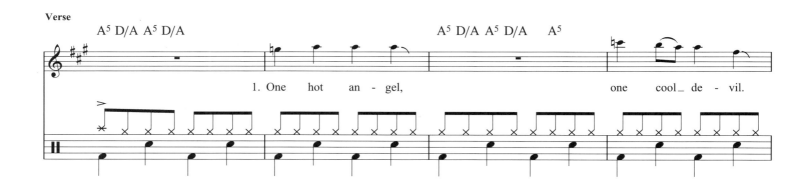

1. One hot an-gel, one cool de-vil.

Your mind on a fan-ta-sy, liv-ing on the ec-sta-sy.

Guitar solo

Verse

closer hats

3. One hot South-ern Belle, son of a de-vil,

a school-boy's spell-ing bee, a school-girl with a fan-ta-sy.

run-a-way train, run-nin' right off the track.

THUNDERSTRUCK

WORDS & MUSIC BY
ANGUS YOUNG & MALCOLM YOUNG

© Copyright 1990 J. Albert & Son Pty. Limited.
All Rights Reserved. International Copyright Secured.

FULL PERFORMANCE DEMO: CD 1 TRACK 10
BACKING ONLY: CD 2 TRACK 10

Intro
2 bar count in:
♩ = 138

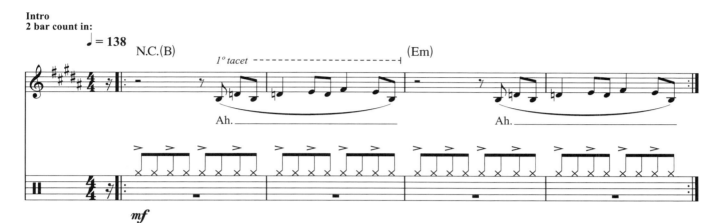

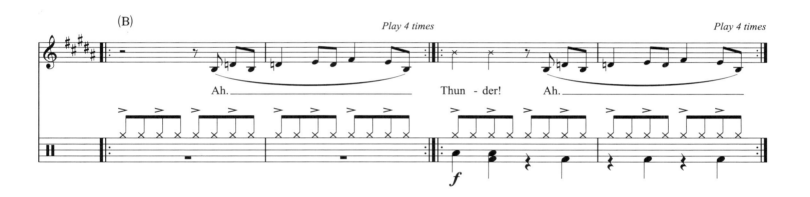

Verse

in the mid - dle of a rail - road track, _____ (Thun - der!) I looked 'round_

(4)

_____ and I knew_____ there was no turn - ing back. (Thun - der!) My mind raced_

(8)

_____ and I thought_____ what_ could I do, _____ (Thun - der!) and I knew_

(12)

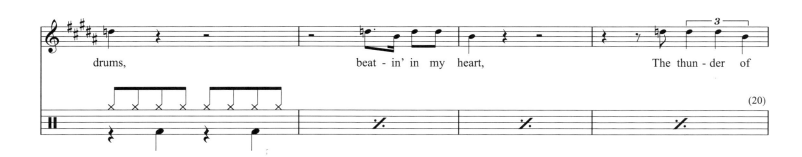

_____ there was no _____ help, no help from you. (Thun - der!) Sound of the

(16)

drums, beat - in' in my heart, The thun - der of

(20)

guns,   yeah,   tore me a - part.

You've been   thun - der struck.

Rode down the

Verse

high - way,_____ broke the li - mit,   we hit the town._____ Went through to

Tex - as,_____   yeah__ Tex - as__ and we had some fun.   We met some

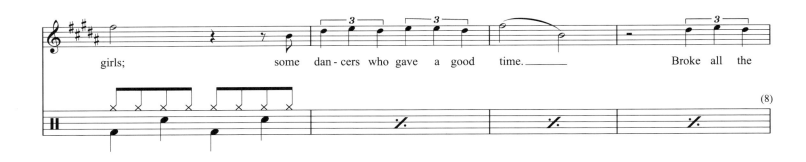

girls; some dan - cers who gave a good time._____ Broke all the

(8)

rules, played all the fools, yeah,_ yeah, they, they, they blew our minds._____

(12)

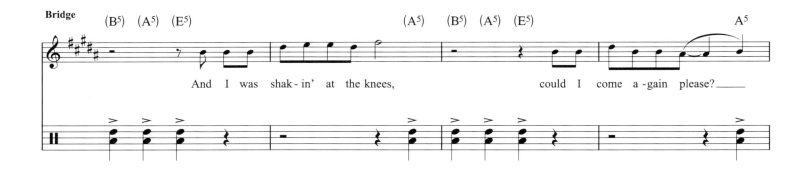

Bridge

(B⁵) (A⁵) (E⁵) (A⁵) (B⁵) (A⁵) (E⁵) A⁵

And I was shak - in' at the knees, could I come a - gain please?_____

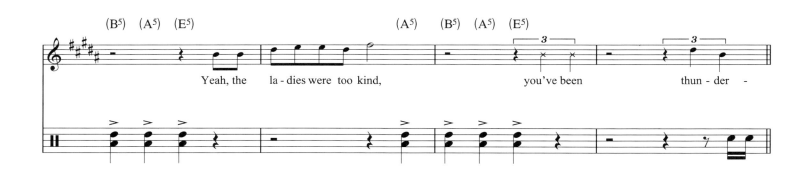

(B⁵) (A⁵) (E⁵) (A⁵) (B⁵) (A⁵) (E⁵)

Yeah, the la - dies were too kind, you've been thun - der -

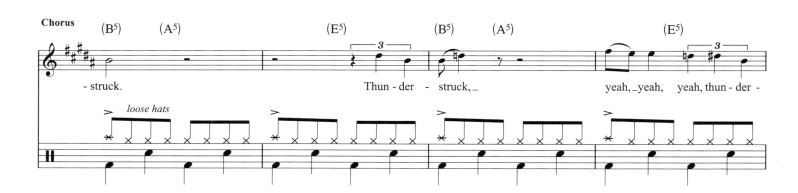

Chorus

(B⁵) (A⁵) (E⁵) (B⁵) (A⁵) (E⁵)

- struck. Thun - der - struck,_ yeah,_ yeah, yeah, thun - der -

loose hats

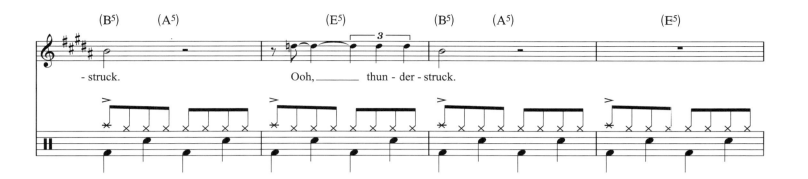

-struck. Ooh,_____ thun - der - struck.

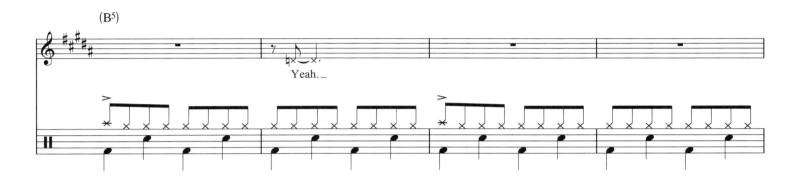

Yeah.__

Ooh, I was shak-ing at the knees,_____ could I come a-gain_ please?_

Gtr. solo

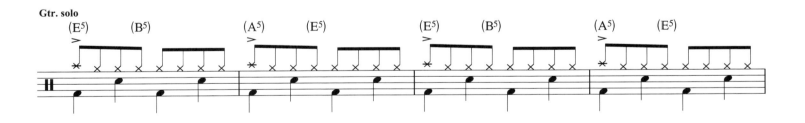

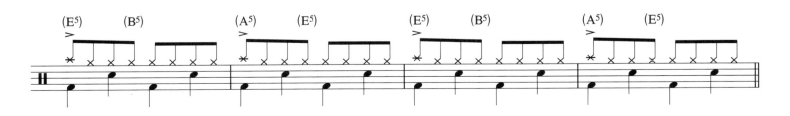

T.N.T.

WORDS & MUSIC BY
ANGUS YOUNG, MALCOLM YOUNG & BON SCOTT

FULL PERFORMANCE DEMO: CD 1 TRACK 11
BACKING ONLY: CD 2 TRACK 11

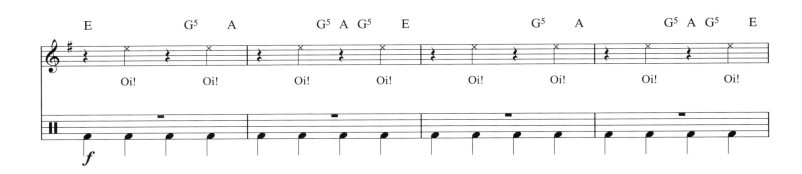

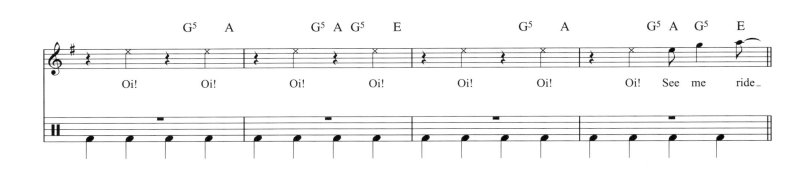

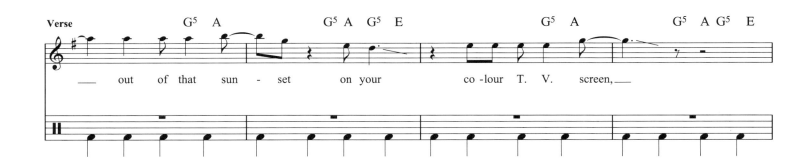

win the fight.___ (T. N. T.) I'm a pow-er load.___

(T. N. T.) Watch me ex - plode.___

I'm

dirt - y, mean and migh-ty un - clean, I'm a want-ed man.___

closed hats

Pub - lic e-ne-my___ num - ber one,___ un-der - stand? So

67

(T. N. T.) Watch me ex - plode.___

Gtr. solo

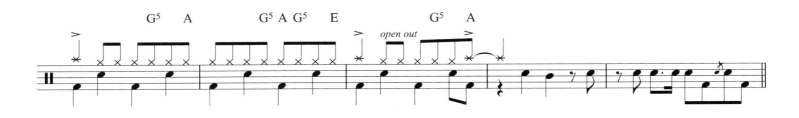

Chorus

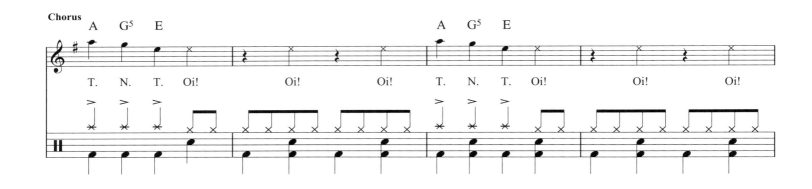

T. N. T. Oi! Oi! Oi! T. N. T. Oi! Oi! Oi!

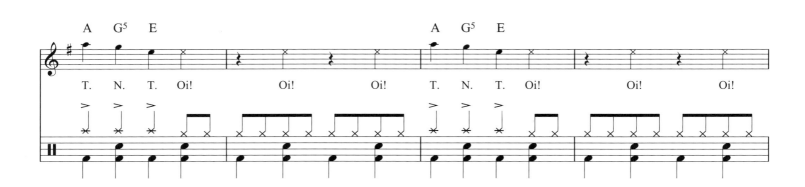

T. N. T. Oi! Oi! Oi! T. N. T. Oi! Oi! Oi!

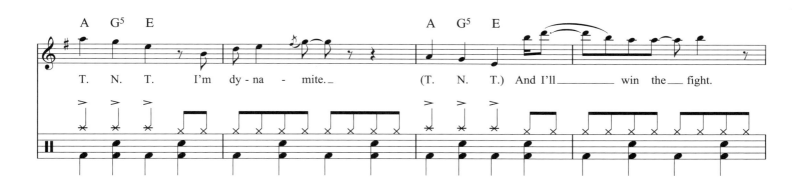

T. N. T. I'm dy-na-mite.__ (T. N. T.) And I'll_____ win the__ fight.

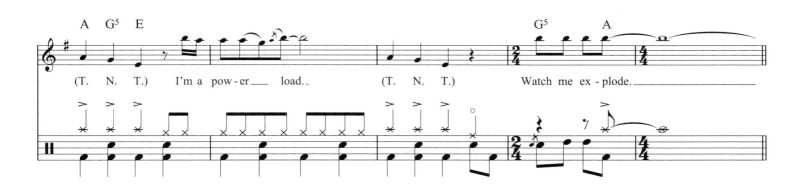

(T. N. T.) I'm a pow-er__ load.__ (T. N. T.) Watch me ex-plode._____

Outro

loose hats

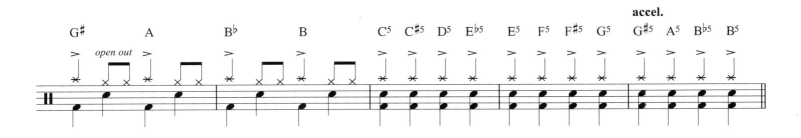

open out

accel.

Free time

ad lib. fill

WHOLE LOTTA ROSIE (LIVE)

WORDS & MUSIC BY
ANGUS YOUNG, MALCOLM YOUNG & BON SCOTT

FULL PERFORMANCE DEMO: CD 1 TRACK 12
BACKING ONLY: CD 2 TRACK 12

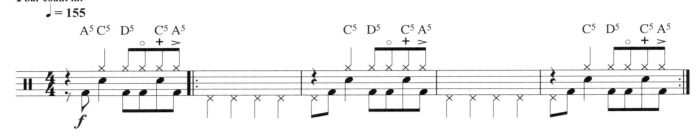

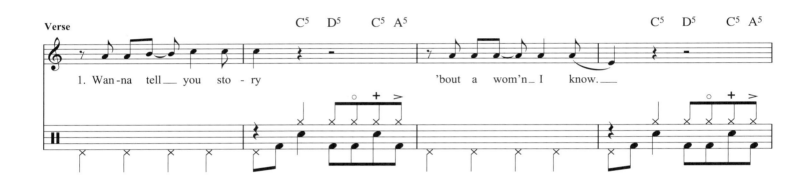

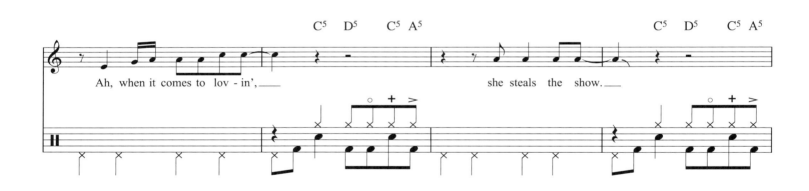

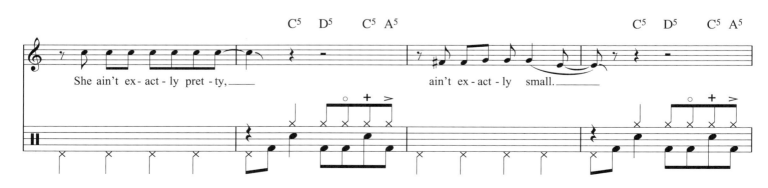

Fort' two, thirt' nine, fif - ty six, you could say she's got a lot.

loose hats

Verse (A⁵)

Nev - er had a wo-man, nev - er had a wo-man like you,___
Ho-ney you can do it, do it to me all night long,___ on -

do - in' all the things, do - in' all the things you do.___
- ly one who turns, on - ly one who turns me on.___

Ain't no fair - y sto - ry, ain't no skin and bones,___ but you
All through the night time and right a - round the clock,___

give it all you got,   weigh-in' in at nine-teen stone.___   You're a whole   lot-ta
to my sur-prise,   Ro - sie nev - er stops. She was a whole   lot-ta

Chorus

F   D⁵

wo-man,   a whole lot - ta wo-man,   a whole lot - ta

A⁵   G⁵   A⁵   G⁵

Ros - ie,   whole lot - ta Ros - ie,   whole lot - ta

1.

A⁵   G⁵   D/F♯   G⁵   D/F♯   G⁵

Ros - ie,   and you're a whole lot - ta wo-man.

A⁵

loose hats

Oh,

72

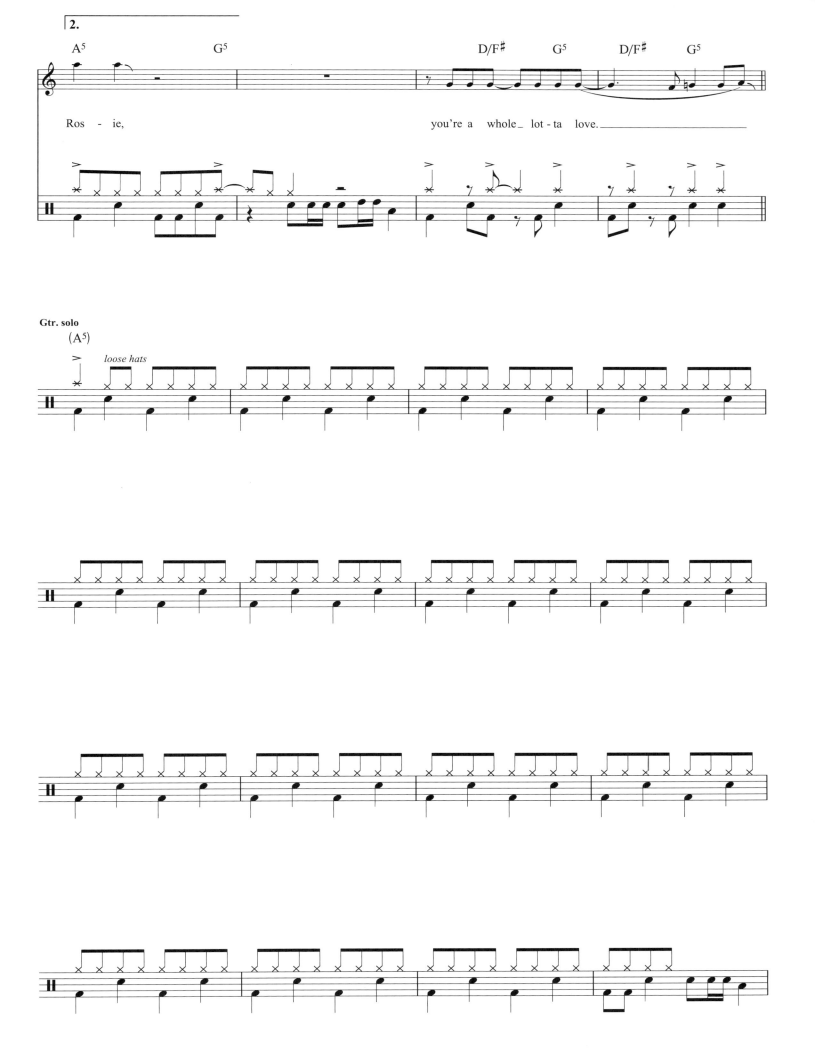

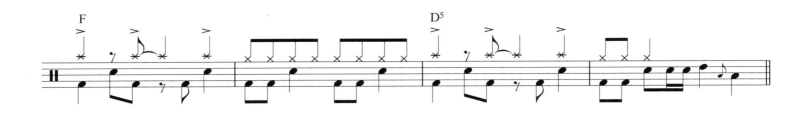

play 5 times

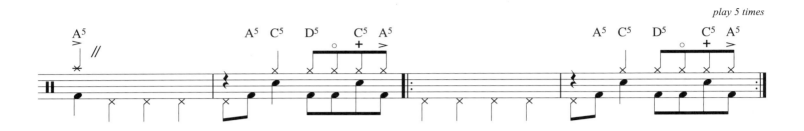

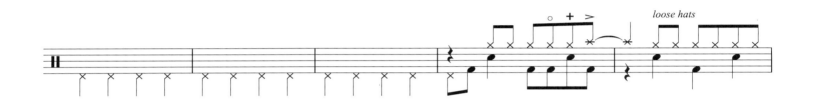

YOU SHOOK ME ALL NIGHT LONG

WORDS & MUSIC BY
ANGUS YOUNG, MALCOLM YOUNG & BRIAN JOHNSON

FULL PERFORMANCE DEMO: CD 1 TRACK 13
BACKING ONLY: CD 2 TRACK 13

Verse
(1.) fast ma-chine,__ she kept her mo-tor clean,__ she was the best damn wo-man that I've
(2.) dou-ble time__ on the se-duc-tion line,__ she was one of a kind, she's just

ev-er seen.__ She had the sight-less eyes__ tell-in' me no lies,__
mine all mine,__ Want-ed no ap-plause__ just an-oth-er course.__ Made a

knock-in' me out__ with those A-mer-i-can thighs. Tak-in' more that her share__ had me
meal out-ta me__ and came back for more. Had to cool me down to take an-

Chorus

CD TRACK LISTING

DISC 1
FULL INSTRUMENTAL PERFORMANCES (WITH DRUMS)...

1. **BACK IN BLACK**
(A. YOUNG/M. YOUNG/B. JOHNSON) J. ALBERT & SON PTY. LTD

2. **DIRTY DEEDS DONE DIRT CHEAP**
(A. YOUNG/M. YOUNG/B. SCOTT) J. ALBERT & SON PTY. LTD.

3. **FOR THOSE ABOUT TO ROCK (WE SALUTE YOU)**
(A. YOUNG/M. YOUNG/B. JOHNSON) J. ALBERT & SON PTY. LTD.

4. **HELLS BELLS**
(A. YOUNG/M. YOUNG/B. JOHNSON) J. ALBERT & SON PTY. LTD.

5. **HIGHWAY TO HELL**
(A. YOUNG/M. YOUNG/B. SCOTT) J. ALBERT & SON PTY. LTD.

6. **IT'S A LONG WAY TO THE TOP (IF YOU WANNA ROCK 'N' ROLL)**
(A. YOUNG/M. YOUNG/B. SCOTT) J. ALBERT & SON PTY. LTD.

7. **LET THERE BE ROCK**
(A. YOUNG/M. YOUNG/B. SCOTT) J. ALBERT & SON PTY. LTD.

8. **ROCK AND ROLL AIN'T NOISE POLLUTION**
(A. YOUNG/M. YOUNG/B. JOHNSON) J. ALBERT & SON PTY. LTD

9. **ROCK 'N' ROLL TRAIN**
(A. YOUNG/M. YOUNG) LEIDSEPLEIN PRESSE B.V.
ADMINISTERED BY J. ALBERT & SON PTY. LTD.

10. **THUNDERSTRUCK**
(A. YOUNG/M. YOUNG) J. ALBERT & SON PTY. LTD.

11. **T.N.T.**
(A. YOUNG/M. YOUNG/B. SCOTT) J. ALBERT & SON PTY. LTD.

12. **WHOLE LOTTA ROSIE (LIVE)**
(A. YOUNG/M. YOUNG/B. SCOTT) J. ALBERT & SON PTY. LTD.

13. **YOU SHOOK ME ALL NIGHT LONG**
(A. YOUNG/M. YOUNG/B. JOHNSON) J. ALBERT & SON PTY. LTD.

DISC 2
BACKING TRACKS (WITHOUT DRUMS)...

1. **BACK IN BLACK**
2. **DIRTY DEEDS DONE DIRT CHEAP**
3. **FOR THOSE ABOUT TO ROCK (WE SALUTE YOU)**
4. **HELLS BELLS**
5. **HIGHWAY TO HELL**
6. **IT'S A LONG WAY TO THE TOP (IF YOU WANNA ROCK 'N' ROLL)**
7. **LET THERE BE ROCK**
8. **ROCK AND ROLL AIN'T NOISE POLLUTION**
9. **ROCK 'N' ROLL TRAIN**
10. **THUNDERSTRUCK**
11. **T.N.T.**
12. **WHOLE LOTTA ROSIE (LIVE)**
13. **YOU SHOOK ME ALL NIGHT LONG**

To remove the CDs from the plastic sleeves,
lift the small lip to break the perforation.
Replace the discs after use for convenient storage.

YAMAHA BAND STUDENT

A BAND METHOD FOR GROUP OR INDIVIDUAL INSTRUCTION

by

Sandy Feldstein
John O'Reilly

Welcome to Book 2 of the YAMAHA BAND STUDENT.

Your completion of Book 1 shows that you have worked hard and made fine progress towards becoming an accomplished musician.

The YAMAHA BAND STUDENT Book 2 will provide you with continued growth in developing a foundation for your future in music: as a composer, rock musician, teacher, conductor, symphony musician, or a listener enjoying the life-long benefits of music.

Your teacher's special skills, a fine instrument, your personal commitment and the YAMAHA BAND STUDENT is all it takes.

Continue your exploration into the world of music; it is YOUR world!

Sandy Feldstein

John O'Reilly

Alfred

YAMAHA®
is a registered trademark of
Yamaha Corporation of America

Instrumentation

Flute
Oboe
Bassoon
Bb Clarinet
Eb Alto Clarinet
Bb Bass Clarinet
Eb Alto Saxophone
Bb Tenor Saxophone
Eb Baritone Saxophone
Bb Trumpet/Cornet
Horn in F
Horn in Eb
Trombone
Baritone T.C.
Baritone B.C.
Tuba
Percussion—S.D., B.D., Access.
Keyboard Percussion
Combined Percussion
Piano Accompaniment
Piano Accompaniment Cassette
Conductor's Score

TENOR SAXOPHONE FINGERING CHART

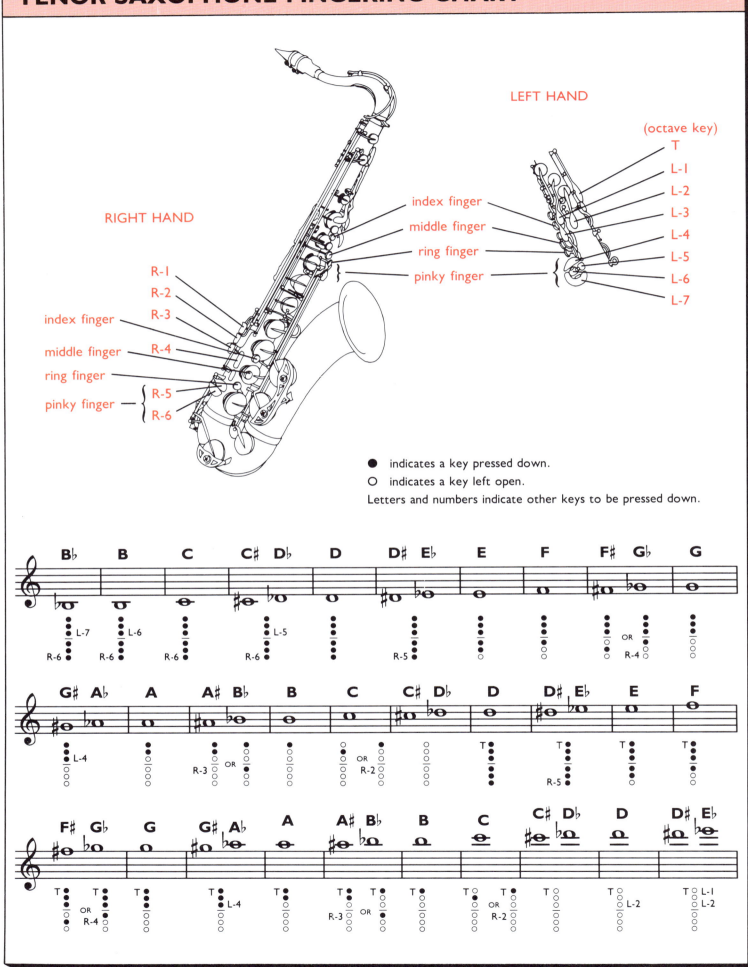

THE PARTS OF THE TENOR SAXOPHONE

ligature — mouthpiece

neck — octave key

neck screw

body

keys

roller

bell section

tone hole — key guard

bow

STUDENT'S PRACTICE CHART

Name _____ To become a good musician you must practice every day. Find a convenient place where you can keep your instrument, book, music stand and any other practice equipment. Try to practice at the same time every day.

Week	MON	TUES	WED	THURS	FRI	SAT	SUN	Approval	Week	MON	TUES	WED	THURS	FRI	SAT	SUN	Approval
1									19								
2									20								
3									21								
4									22								
5									23								
6									24								
7									25								
8									26								
9									27								
10									28								
11									29								
12									30								
13									31								
14									32								
15									33								
16									34								
17									35								
18									36								

4

KEY SIGNATURE REVIEW

G Major (F Major Concert)   **C Major** (Bb Major Concert)   **F Major** (Eb Major Concert)

G Major Scale and Chords
(F Major Concert)

1

Michael, Row the Boat Ashore

2 Moderato

C Major Scale and Chords
(Bb Major Concert)

3

Deck the Halls

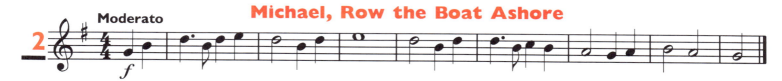

4 Allegro

F Major Scale and Chords
(Eb Major Concert)

5

Carnival of Venice

6 Vivo

Key Signature Review

Fill in your key name, draw your clef, and complete the key signature.

Concert Key	My Key	Key Signature	Concert Key	My Key	Key Signature	Concert Key	My Key	Key Signature
F Major	_____		Bb Major	_____		Eb Major	_____	

SYNCOPATION

D.C. al Coda (Da Capo al Coda)

Go back to the beginning,
play to ⊕ then skip to the coda.

Liza Jane

Alleluia

MOZART

Syncopated Duo

Duet

D.C. al Coda

⊕ *Coda*

D.C. al Coda

⊕ *Coda*

High Flyer March

The Streets of Laredo

Pomp and Circumstance
Duet

ELGAR

Just for Saxophones

Alternate Fingering

*= Alternate C fingering

B♭ Major Scale and Chords
(A♭ Major Concert)

Manhattan Beach
SOUSA

Give My Regards to Broadway
COHAN

D.C. al Coda

Coda

Add the Bar Lines—Then Clap the Rhythm

8

B♭ Major Scale Study
(A♭ Major Concert)

1

Yankee Doodle Dandy

COHAN

2

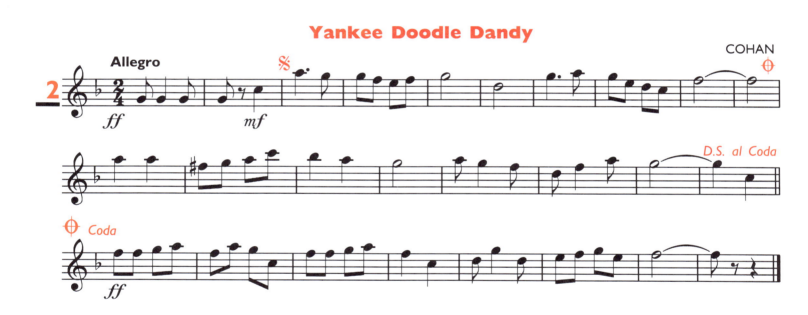

Dot-Dash Blues
Duet

3

4

FULL BAND ARRANGEMENT

A Joyful Chorale

J. S. BACH
Arranged by
SANDY FELDSTEIN and JOHN O'REILLY

Maple Leaf March

SANDY FELDSTEIN
and JOHN O'REILLY

RITARDANDO

rit. or *ritard.*
slow down

A TEMPO

return to tempo
(used after *rit.*)

Trumpet Voluntary

CLARKE

Angels We Have Heard on High

Duet

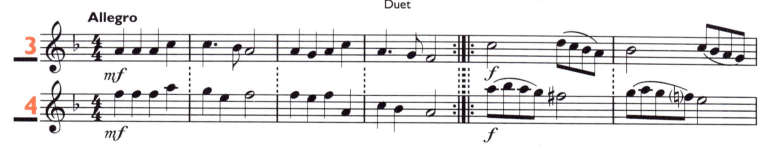

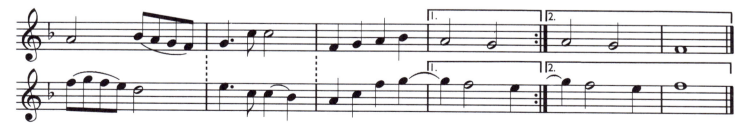

**Just for
Saxophones**

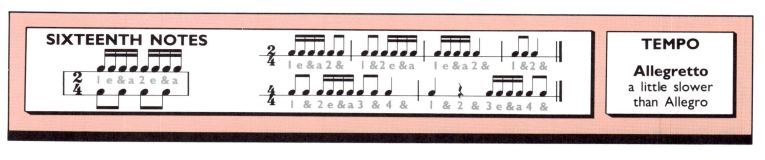

The Thunderer

SOUSA

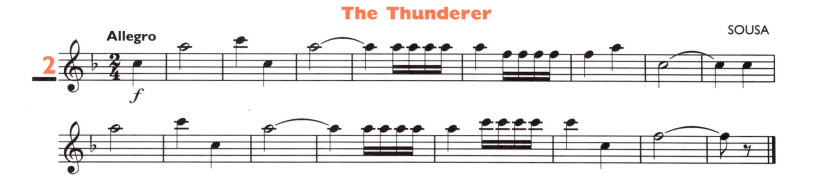

Morning Has Broken

Listen to the Mockingbird

Add the Missing Notes—Then Clap the Rhythm

The Minstrel Boy

The High School Cadets

SOUSA

Nobody Knows the Trouble I've Seen

Dueling Sixteenths

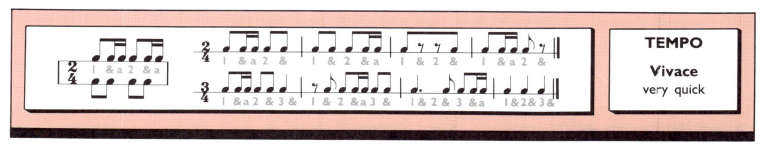

TEMPO

Vivace
very quick

D Major Scale and Chords
(C Major Concert)

American Patrol

MEACHAM

Merry Widow Waltz

LEHAR

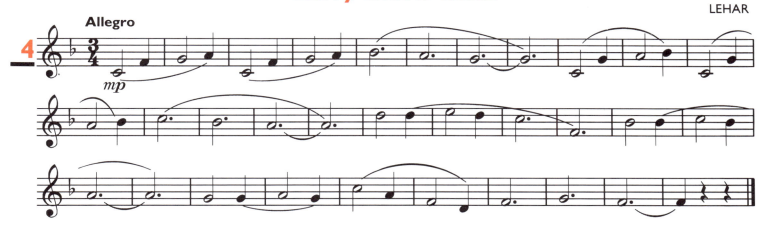

Theme from the William Tell Overture

ROSSINI

D Major Scale Study

(C Major Concert)

Little Brown Jug

Skip to My Lou

Just for Saxophones

B♭

Alternate Fingering

*=Alternate fork fingering B♭

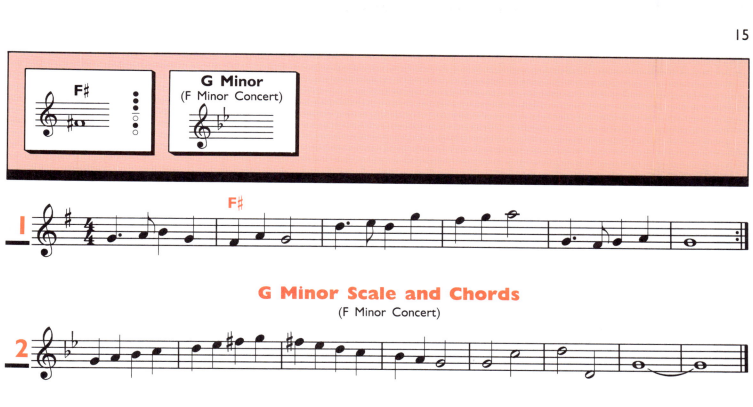

G Minor Scale and Chords
(F Minor Concert)

Greensleeves

Clapping Sixteenths
Hand Clap Duet

A Little Pop
Duet

FULL BAND ARRANGEMENT

Hallelujah Chorus
from "Messiah"

G. F. HANDEL
Arranged by SANDY FELDSTEIN
and JOHN O'REILLY

ACCELERANDO

gradually
get faster

F Technic Study
(E♭ Concert)

Theme from March Slav

TCHAIKOVSKY

This Old Man
Duet

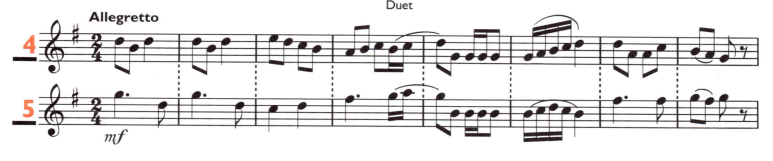

Just for Saxophones

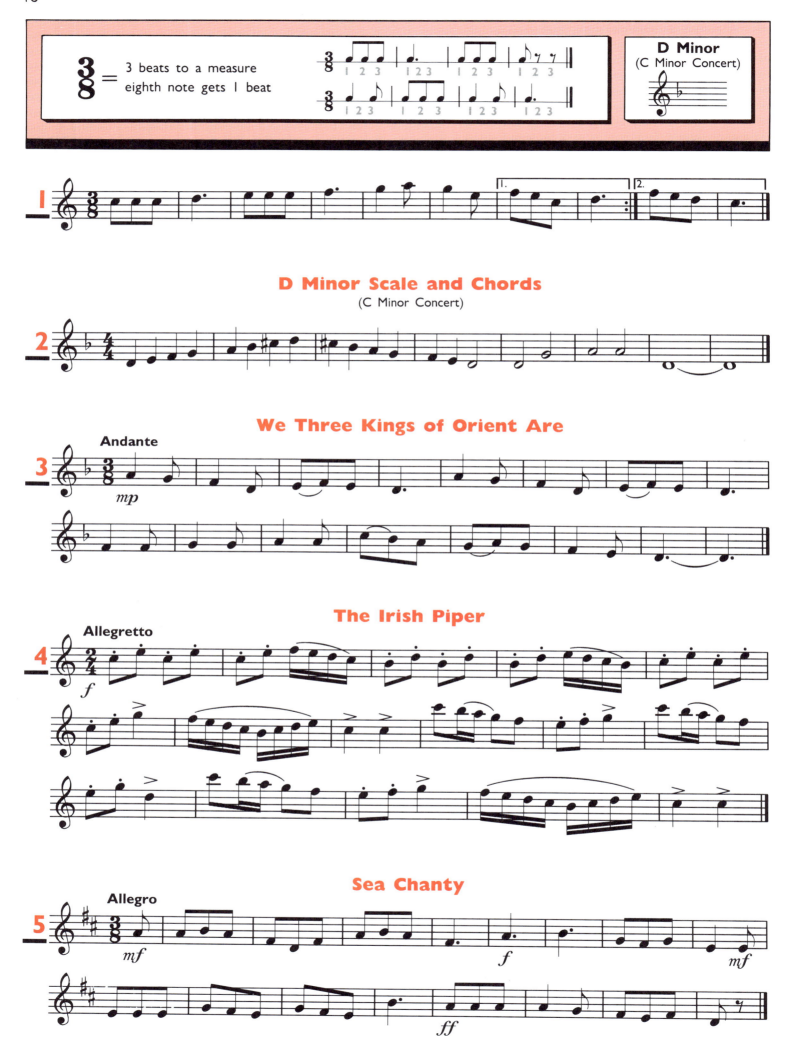

D Minor
(C Minor Concert)

D Minor Scale and Chords
(C Minor Concert)

We Three Kings of Orient Are

The Irish Piper

Sea Chanty

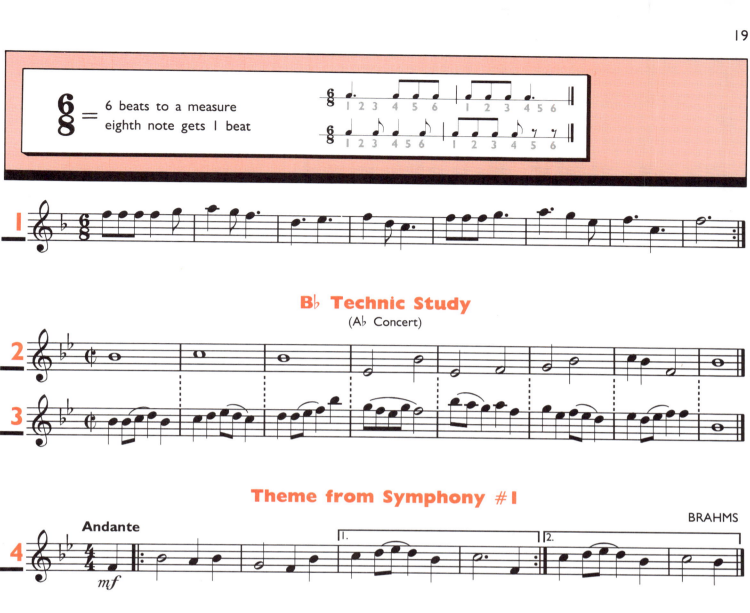

B♭ Technic Study
(A♭ Concert)

Theme from Symphony #1

BRAHMS

Skipping Along
Duet

Add the Bar Lines—Then Clap the Rhythm

ENHARMONIC NOTES

Two notes that sound the same but are written differently.

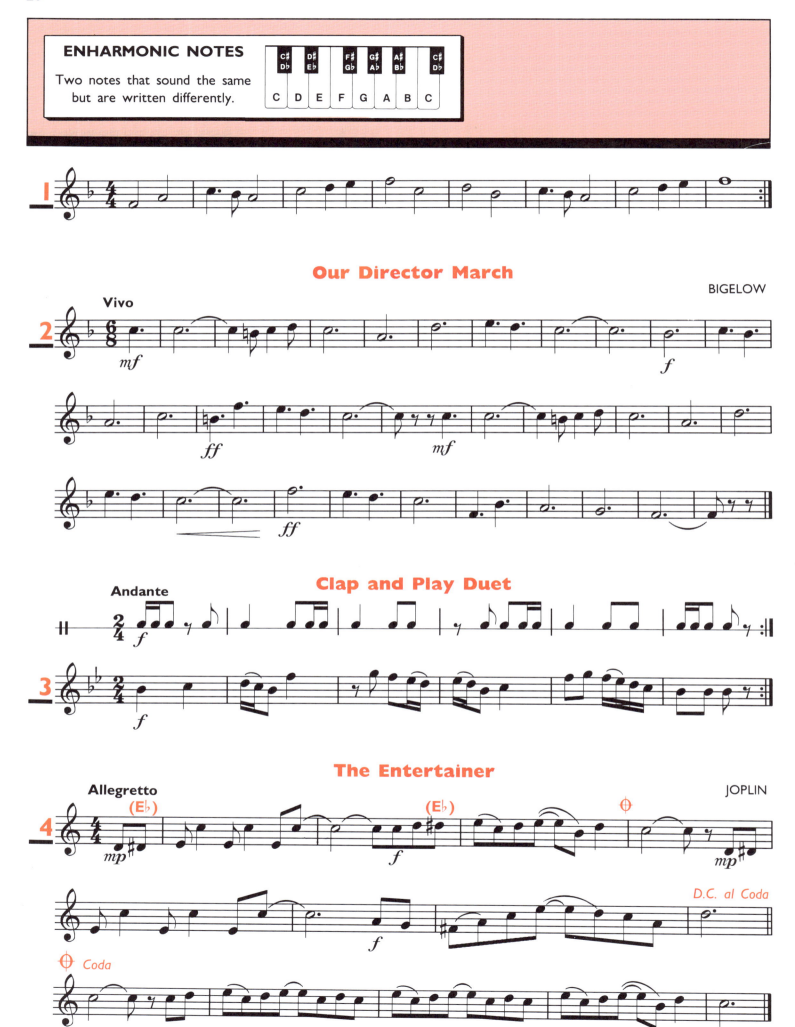

Our Director March

BIGELOW

Clap and Play Duet

The Entertainer

JOPLIN

D.C. al Coda

Coda

E Minor (D Minor Concert)

TEMPO

Presto very fast

E Minor Scale and Chords
(D Minor Concert)

Three Blind Mice
Round

Allegro

Russian Sailor's Dance

Moderato

Sweet Betsy from Pike

Presto

Just for Saxophones

F#

Alternate Fingerings

*=Chromatic F# fingering

Our Boys Will Shine Tonight

The Yellow Rose of Texas

A Touch of Blue
Duet

Rhythm Addition
Answer each problem with only one note.

FULL BAND ARRANGEMENT

Stargazer Overture

SANDY FELDSTEIN
and JOHN O'REILLY

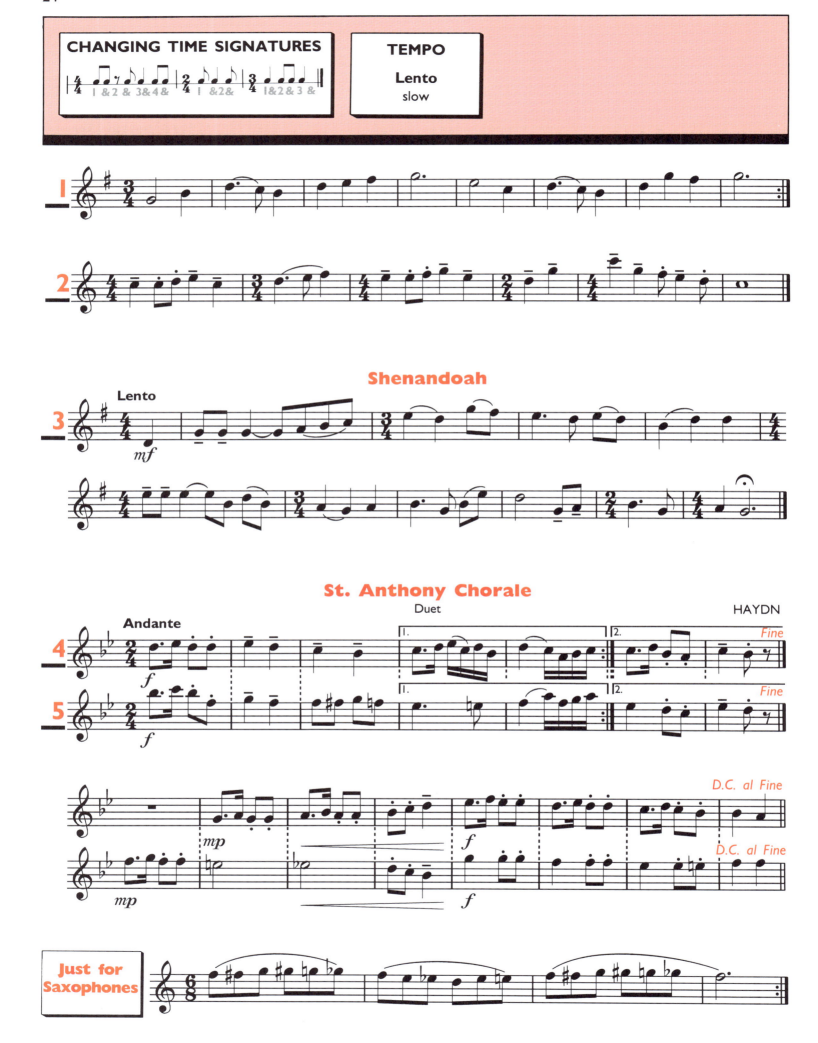

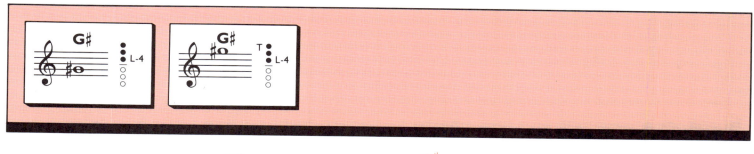

D Technic Study
(C Concert)

Soldier's March

SCHUMANN

The Stars and Stripes Forever

SOUSA

26

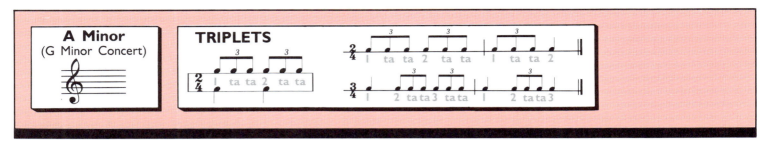

A Minor Scale and Chords
(G Minor Concert)

Semper Fidelis

SOUSA

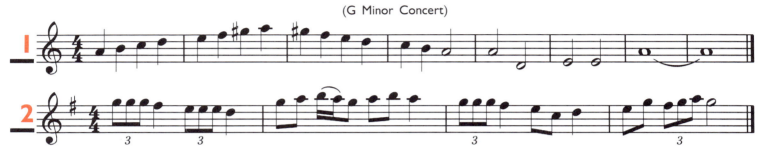

Theme from Farandole

BIZET

Triumphal March from Aida

VERDI

Key Signature Review

Fill in your key name, draw your clef, and complete the key signature.

Concert Key	My Key	Key Signature	Concert Key	My Key	Key Signature	Concert Key	My Key	Key Signature	Concert Key	My Key	Key Signature
F Minor			D Minor			E Minor			G Minor		

CHROMATIC SCALE

A chromatic scale uses all 12 musical notes.

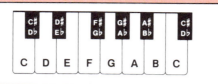

Chromatic Scale Study

March from the Nutcracker Ballet

TCHAIKOVSKY

Here We Come A Wassailing

Movin' On Blues

Duet

Bill Bailey

Pop Goes the Weasel

He's Got the Whole World in His Hands

Hungarian Dance

BRAHMS

FULL BAND ARRANGEMENT

Blues Rock Finale

SANDY FELDSTEIN
and JOHN O'REILLY

TENOR SAXOPHONE SOLO

Minuet

L. VAN BEETHOVEN

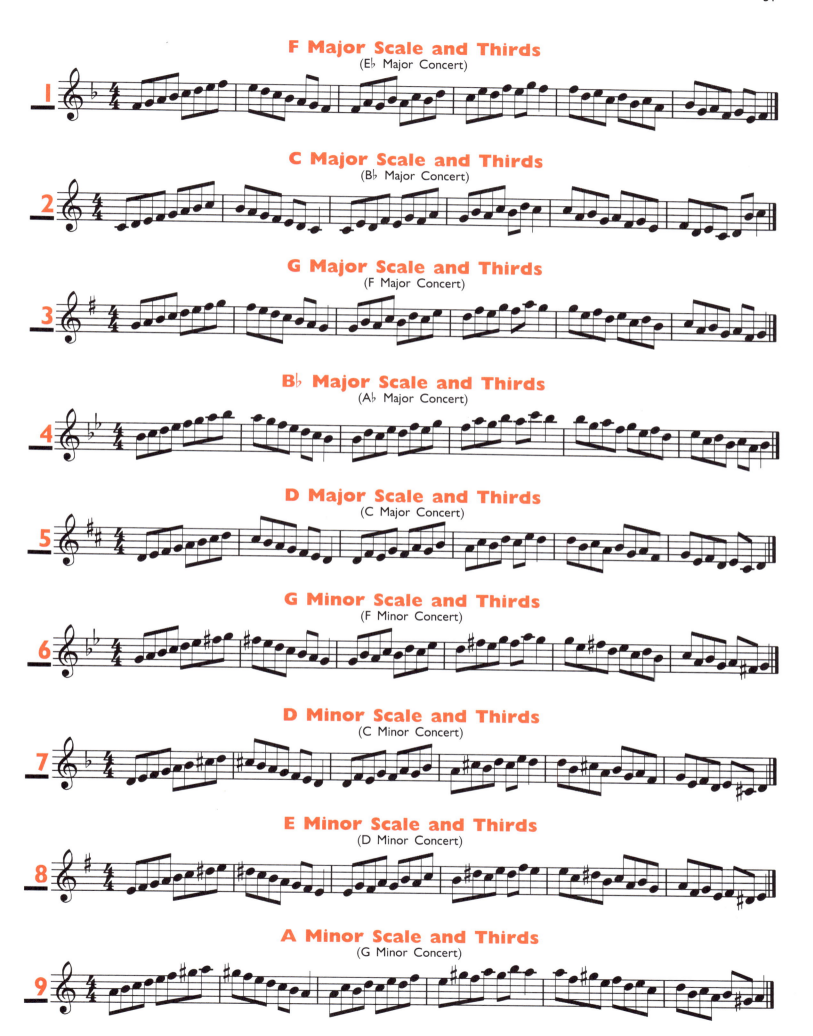

YAMAHA BAND STUDENT

CERTIFICATE
OF ACHIEVEMENT

YAMAHA BAND STUDENT

has successfully completed Book Two of the
Yamaha Band Student and is promoted to Book Three.

_____
Band Director

Date

_____
Authors